# Seven Articles

# Concerning Government and Health Care

by

**Kerry R. Scott**

## Contents:

# "Draining the Swamp"

by

Kerry R. Scott

03/07/2017

I have followed with interest the political roller-coaster that has been going on in Washington for the last three months. As you already know President Trump is not my favorite person and was not my favorite candidate for President (Marco Rubio holding that position in my mind), but Trump is now the President and I do feel that we owe the person who holds that position at least the respect that the position itself demands.

Although the American people elects a "person" for the position of President and that person has a particular personality type, which may or may not be likable for all sections of the population, it is the policies of that President that determines his position on the political spectrum. This essay, however, is not about the political spectrum – it is not about whether President Trump's policies are Republican or Democrat. In fact I do not think that President Trump, although he ran on the Republican ticket, is, in fact, a true Republican and he is certainly not a Democrat. His whole governing objective seem to have nothing to do with politics and his sole reason and plan for governing is simply to make "America Great Again".

I need to digress a little here to make my point. In his book, *The Practice of Management*, first published in 1954, Peter Drucker described a technique of management that he called *Management by Objectives*. As can be expected since 1954 this technique has been developed, adjusted and updated. One particular adjustment that was of significant interest to this writer was during the 70's when a version of this technique was developed for the Non-profit organization and membership organizations. It was primarily developed for the fund-raising projects for such organizations but was equally applicable to personnel and inventory management and organization.

Simply put *Management by Objectives* sets a general **Goal** or **Mission,** then applies a series of **Objectives** that lead to the possible fulfilling the **Goal** or completing the **Mission**. A series of **Strategies** are then developed in order to complete each of the **Objectives** and lastly a flexible **"time-line"** is set. Built into the system is a series of evaluation points that can change the whole nature of the plan if new **Objectives** appear or one or more of the **Objectives** are not achieved.

End of digression.

It has been stated to me a number of times that President Trump has no hope for being a successful President as he is trying to run the Government as a business and that is not possible. Humbly, I submit that the government is a "business". A very large and amorphous "business" and perhaps operating under a Non-profit business plan but nevertheless it still should be considered a "business" and should be administered as such.

If we try and apply Management by Objectives techniques to President Donald Trump's governing actions it can be assumed that *"Making America Great Again"* could be considered his **Goal** or **Mission.** This was my first thought but then after some serious pondering I realized that if this phrase was a goal then it would be written "To Make America Great Again". The phrase written *"Making America Great Again"* was an action phrase and represented the **"Result"** of reaching a successful **Goal** rather than the **Goal** itself.  This realization gave rise to the question as to the identity of the **Goal**.

Prior to the election the one thing that the majority of Americans (Democrats, Republicans and Independents et.al) could all agree upon was that "Washington was broken" and that they needed a President that could break with tradition and clean up the mess in which the Federal Government found itself. This eventually led to the "Trump Supporters" coining the phrase *"Draining the Swamp"*.

The culture of Washington is, most probably, more corrupt than any American can imagine. All Americans are aware that all is not well in our Federal Government but few are really aware of how bad the situation has become. In no small part this is because for the last decade the party in power believed that Government was the answer to all problems, that the larger the Government the more effective it was and there was no part of our individual lives that cannot be controlled and "helped" by Government.

*"Draining the Swamp"* therefore becomes a five tier rout. Firstly the elected positions need to be replaced with educated and enlightened candidates and candidates that will do their constituent's wishes and not make the spurious excuse of "following their conscience". Secondly, the politically appointed positions should be based on experience and ability to perform the tasks associated with the particular position and not let their partisan aspirations interfere with their performing of their duties. Thirdly, Federal workers should only hold an ongoing position if, based on their work ethic and standard of performance, they warrant keeping the position. Fourthly lobbying, lobbyists and Lobbying Companies should be outlawed. Fifthly, Unions representing any Federal associated workers should be forbidden.

From the above I would submit that the **Goal** of President Trump's agenda is indeed *"Draining the Swamp"* and his **Objectives** (those stepping-stone programs designed to achieve the **Goal**) are as follows:

1. Bringing jobs back to the USA.
2. Repealing and renewing American Health Care.

3. Revising the tax system.
4. Revising the immigration system.
5. Securing the borders.

The process of making the above **Objectives** succeed will, by definition, require removing the culture of corruption that exists in Washington. Little by little, item by item, the dross, the incompetent and the inept will be removed from the culture as each of the items above are accomplished making the next one easier to achieve. It is only after all the items above are processed that the full extent of the "Swamp" will be made clear and as each item is tackled so the "Swamp" members can be identified and eliminated.

In other words, while President Trump continues to bring to the fore his promises he made during his campaign, he hi-lights the various inadequacies of the personnel of the Federal Government in Washington and forces a scrutiny of the obviously corrupt processes of Government. While his promises may or may not come to fruition he exposes and makes public, corrupt policies that have, up to now, gone unnoticed and affected in secret.

We have seen a number of examples of this ethically motivated clean-up. Almost in tandem with the President's policy proposals and obviously because of the scrutiny created by the proposals the public has been made aware of the following corruption perpetrated by various members of the Government.

1. The "Fourth Estate" were the first culprits exposed for creating false reports. This they continue to do paying no attention to the "truth" of their stories. The Media were closely followed by the Intelligence Agencies which could not seem to get their stories straight and in the end cowered under the "Classified" excuse.
2. Next came the Republican Party (particularly the Speaker of the House). Republicans managed to be make a series of poor judgments concerning the Health Care Bill and were exposed as a divided party that even after years of planning could not come up with a Bill that was even acceptable to their own party. The Bill, however, did not fail but was withdrawn and it is being reported that The American Health Care Bill is now being revised to a form that it can smoothly become the law of the land. Although, perhaps, being used as a scapegoat, the Speaker of the House is not leading the revision but rather the Vice President is taking on that role. Perhaps this is the change that will salvage the reputation of the Republican Congress members by exposing those members that are ineffective and not working toward "*Making America Great Again*".
3. Congress and Senate Committees on Intelligence both have been shown as ineffective and riddled with back-biting and uncivil behavior.
4. The Senate, out of simple vengeance and spite, are ready to try and block a supremely qualified and experienced Supreme Court nominee by forcing a Senate rule that has existed for over one hundred years to be changed; and thus forcing setting a precedent that cannot be changed and will have far reaching negative ramifications for both parties.

5.   The Federal Courts and individual Federal Judges themselves are being exposed for trying to ignore the Constitutional "separation of powers"  and not only trying to legislate from the "bench" but becoming rogue Courts and Judges by making this legislation partisan in nature.

Ultimately it is the American public that will determine whether this corrupt behavior is acceptable anywhere but particularly in Washington. When the very essence of society is so thoroughly corrupt, when the people's Government cannot be trusted and when there is no recourse to the law to right the wrongs perpetrated upon society, then, history has taught us, that the only recourse for the people is "revolution". When has "revolution" ever solved of made better society's ills?

From what I have observed President Trump is a "big picture guy". He knows what he wants to accomplish and then sets up a team to achieve that particular **Objective**. A good example of this was the American Health Care Bill. Although the President supported the bill – it was not a bill that was initiated by the President – it was a Republican bill – badly written, badly presented and really having no redeeming feature, perhaps – but not a bill that fully filled the promises made by the then Candidate Trump during the Presidential Campaign. So why did the President let the bill be presented? Why did he support the bill? Why did he immediately move onto something else once the bill was withdrawn? The answer to those questions, I believe, is that as far as the President is concerned there ware two **Strategies** in play.

Firstly, President Trump wanted, with his first foray into legislation, to "test the waters". That is, to find out what was necessary to insure successful legislation and what the pitfalls were in dealing with the Congress, the Republican Party and to a lesser extent what the Democrats plans were. This was risky policy, but it must be remembered that this was not the President's bill – it belonged to the Congressional Republicans and as such if it failed, it would provide much needed information on the dynamics of the process of legislation led by the Republicans. If on the other hand it was successful it would be a great first step on the repeal and replace of American Health Care legislation.

Secondly, (and I believe more important to President Trump than the first point) it exposed and "laid bare" the corrupt approach of Congress to a piece of legislation that was universally requested by the American people. It exposed the laughable approach to passing a Bill, it made clear the partisan approach of individual representatives as well as splits in the Republican party on ideological lines and how far the individual Congress members would go to ignore the wishes of their constituents. Lastly it made clear the power and influence the lobbyists and special interest groups could leverage onto congress to obtain their own requirements.

We know that President Trump is a "pragmatist" and not an "ideologue". If we add to that the concept that President Trump is also a "big picture guy" we can surmise that the success or defeat of any single **Objective** does not alter his course of action and does not make much of difference to the way he is thinking. If all of his promises to his supporters (agenda) fail but the process of legislating those **Objectives** expose the corruption within the government and that corruption is either legislated out of existence or elected out of existence, President Trump will I believe, consider himself successful because he will have achieved his **Goal** and *"drained the swamp"*.

One of the most misunderstood ("misunderestimated") aspects concerning President Trump is that not only is he a "big picture guy" but he cares little about the "details". He will generally support a bill (American Health Care Bill) but will not get into the details. He will indicate that the Obama Administration surveilled his campaign for President, but will not provide back-up details of the surveillance. He will set up the process of building a secure border wall but will not provide any details concerning the design, how long it will take to construct and how it will be funded (other than to indicate Mexico will eventually take on the cost burden). I believe he considers these "details" as inconsequential. He does not care what for instance the wall looks like or how long it takes or in fact how the funds are provided. He has done part of his job concerning "Keeping America Safe" by initiating the building of the wall – and has appointed personnel to deal with the details. President Trump is now moving on with the next **Objective** on his list.

It is quite clear to me that the Washington political culture is decadent, chaotic and amoral. It is dysfunctional and for the last eight years has progressively become more entrenched in corruption. Anything goes in the name of progress.

The Islamic world characterizes the whole Western Culture as decadent and amoral. I do not believe that this characterization is, in fact, correct but I do see how they come to this conclusion. Islam has set rigid standards in their theocracy to which they obsessively adhere. In their world "truth" is a "reality" that is not a servant of "situational ethics". Recently even the Christian religion has in many cases joined the Progressive's opposite approach, whereby "Truth" is relative to one's individual thoughts, concepts and actions. The Progressives believe that your thoughts are sacrosanct because they are yours alone and not subject to the rule of law, morality norms or the opinions or thoughts of others: absolute Hubris! It is this thought process that leads to the corruption within the Federal Government, the division within the electorate and the angst that pervades the whole population.

I do believe that most Americans understand and will follow the actions of Washington even if they do not completely agree with the terms of the actions or the actions do not appear to impact them directly. However that is not to say most Americans understand the process of legislation. For at least the last eight years the "means justify the ends" mantra seems to have been followed by all those that are part of the Government regardless of their party affiliation. The process of legislation is characterized as "sausage making" and it is a sad statement on the government of a Constitutional Democratic Republic that the process of legislation is likened to the process of making an animal offal food product. The Legislators should be elected by an informed and educated electorate that should understand the legislative process. The Legislative process should, therefore, be an open and transparent operation. It can be, and occasionally should be, passionate and even adversarial but never secretive underhanded, and resorting to bribery.

 A Society is only as strong as the bond between the individual members of that Society and for that bond to remain strong there must be "trust" between members. I am not at all sure that members of the Federal Government trust each other or those constituents they represent.

Respectfully Submitted

Kerry R. Scott

# "Third Time Lucky

## Or

# Three Strikes and You Are Out"

by

Kerry R. Scott

04/28/2017

As the second attempt to revamp the Health Care Act continues I am reminded of two conflicting vernacular sayings: *"Third Time Lucky"* and *"Three Strikes and You Are Out"*. Which one of those sage but over used terms, *"wins the day"* will have to wait until the third attempt to pass Health Care Legislation is undertaken and will be dependent upon how the learning curve of President Trump develops with regard to passing legislation successfully through Congress. (see previous essay "Draining The Swamp")

The single most argued point concerning the involvement of the Federal Government in Health Care is whether there is a Constitutional requirement that the population of the USA has an entitlement to adequate and appropriate Health Care. The Constitution's Preamble says the federal government was established to:

*"form a more perfect union, establish Justice, insure domestic Tranquillity, provide for the common defence, promote the general Welfare, and secure the Blessings of Liberty to ourselves and our Posterity."*

The first clause of Article I, Section 8, however, indicates:

*"The Congress shall have Power to lay and collect Taxes, Duties, Imposts and Excises, to pay the Debts and provide for the common Defence and general Welfare of the United States."*

This clause, often referred to as the *"General Welfare Clause"* or the *"Spending Power Clause"*, does not provide Congress with the power to legislate for the *"general welfare of the country"*; that power is provided for the states through the Tenth Amendment. Rather, it marks a difference between the concepts of *"general Welfare"* and the infinite needs of the *"general welfare of the population of the Nation"*.

It can therefore be argued either, that the Federal Government may have a role to play in the Health Care of Americans or alternatively it may be the individual States that have this responsibility. The term *"promote the general Welfare"*, however, can be interpreted to indicate that anything that impacts the well being of Americans could become the responsibility of the Federal Government.

This argument concerning the interpretation of the meaning "general welfare of the Country" raged for over 150 years and it was only in 1936 that the Supreme Court struck down a Federal spending program that was for the "general welfare of the Country" indicating that it invaded the States rights as indicated by the Tenth Amendment. Although the Supreme Court found for the "limited government" philosophy it also established that the determination of "general welfare" was left to the discretion of Congress.

An *"Originalist"* or *"Textualist"* such as Supreme Court Justice Antonin Scalia or the new Supreme Court Justice Neil Gorsuch, might have a different interpretation of the term *"general Welfare"*: arguing that when the Constitution was written it would never have occurred to the Framers that the tem *"general Welfare"* could have applied to specialist medical techniques such as are available today. Furthermore, it would have been assumed by the Framers that the term *Health Care* would only apply to those people ill or disabled and therefore *"Preventative Health Care"* would not come under the purview of the Federal Government.

Recently, locally we have had an activist make a presentation concerning the Health Care Industry and in particular, expounding the advantages of the *"Single Payer System"*. What is the *"Single Payer System"*? There is considerable misinformation and disinformation concerning the *"Single Payer System"* but in effect it means that the cost of a national health care system is spread over the whole population with compulsory individual payments made directly to the Government via the payroll. Therefore the argument for the system is that all members of the population that contribute to the system can receive health care.

As a Permanent Resident in America (Legal Immigrant), originally from England, a Polio Survivor and a sufferer of Post Polio Syndrome, I have experienced both the "Single Payer System" as well as the system that relies on a Health Care Industry. I have never for my whole life paid anything for my medical expenses. These included a number of significant surgeries, long hospital stays, the wearing of braces for my legs for my whole life and for the production of a power wheelchair for the last six years.

Most of my surgeries and hospital stays occurred in my youth when I resided in England and under a *"single payer system"*. In England this system is called the *"National Health Service"*. It is important to note this national government program is called a *"service"*. It is not an *"industry"* and is not designed to be a profit making endeavor.

The *"National Health Service"* is part of the umbrella governmental system called the *"Welfare State"*. The *"Welfare State"* began to be mooted as an idea during the 1830's by the contemporary Victorian liberals. The concept of a welfare state developed over a period of about 100 years morphing and expanding until it now comprises of expenditures by the UK government that are  intended to improve health, education, employment and social security.  In

1942 the Beveridge Report , (which identified five "Giant Evils" in society: squalor, ignorance, want, idleness and disease) essentially recommended a national, compulsory, flat rate payment scheme which would combine health care, unemployment and retirement benefits. Today these payments are based on salary, but are a separate payment made via the individual payroll to that of the income tax payment.

There are many complaints and objections to the UK *"National Health Service"* including but not limited to "long wait lists for surgeries", "wait lists being adjusted to the detriment of the elderly", "lack of 'cutting edge' medical techniques", "cost determination of procedure necessity", "lack of access to adequate medications" and "poor doctor access". From the above, however, it can be seen that these complaints are to do with the way the system is administered rather than a critique of the concept itself of a "National Health Service". The local activist referred to above, as an advocate of an American *"single payer"* health care system, indicated that the problems indicated in the UK *"National Health Service"* were the result of an "underfunding of the UK system". I am not at all sure that providing increased funding will make any difference to the UK *"National Health Service"*. The system is, in my opinion, administrative heavy, with medical personnel being promoted to administrative positions, therefore reducing the access of the population to qualified medical personnel. However the main problem with the system is that the population of the UK is over 65 million people and it is, in my opinion, impossible to administer and serve that many people centrally. This is so even with the local Health Care Authorities.

One of the main proclamations when The Affordable Health Care Act was first presented was that "you can keep your doctor" or "Have a choice of doctors". The UK *"National Health Service"* does not give the consumer a choice of doctors. All "Primary Care Physicians" ("General Practitioners" – in English NHS speak) are hired by the Government at a fixed indexed salary and assigned to a particular medical parish – that is an geographical area with a particular break down of population (a certain percentage of Children, elderly, handicapped and disabled etc.). As a national Health consumer your doctor will see you when you are sick and if he or she cannot help your ailment then you will be referred to a specialist.

*"Preventative Health Care"* is, therefore, not a large part or of any great importance in the UK *National Health Service* – in the UK one goes to the doctor when one feels unwell and is diagnosed and treated in the appropriate manner. The idea of a *"Preventative Health Care"* system determining the risk factor of developing any particular illness or disease by statistics is a spurious concept for most UK medical professionals: it is simply a method by which the *"economy"* and *"profit margin"* of an *"industry"* can remain viable. Although, as a *"service"* the *"economy"* of the UK *"National Health Service"* is of import, the "profit margin" is a pointless concept. The Income to the UK *"National Health Service"* is not dependent upon Premiums or sales or even the quality of the service it offers, but is secured by the Government. It requires no "quality assurance" and a consumer of the National Health Service cannot "shop around" for a better deal. You get what you are given!

Although Government programs in the UK do have Government oversight they are, of course, subject to partisan politics. This is the same for complaints toward the National Health Service and in many cases much noise is made about abuses while little is actually resolved or remedied. I am reminded of the Veterans Administration where much is made of the problems of Veterans Health Care but improvements come very slowly if at all.

If a "single payer" of health care system was to be instituted in the USA by the Federal Government it would mean that eventually it would, I believe, begin to develop all the problems that I have outlined above in the UK system and as presently evidenced in the American Veterans Administration Health Care system.

I have pointed out that a centrally administered "*Single Payer System*" like the UK "*National Health Service*" has serious problems when it tries to serve a population of 64 million people. As of 2015 the population of the USA is 321 million. If a centralized system of health Care cannot work for a population of 64 million, even with the extra ability, fortitude and exceptionalism of the American Federal Government, can it really be a realistic expectation that this system will work with 321 million consumers. Simply from a realistic and practical point of view I do believe that Congress should use its "discretion" in passing a Health Care Bill on the side of the Tenth Amendment .

There is already an example of a State "single payer" system in operation in Massachusetts. MassHealth was introduced in 2008 and revised in 2010, 2012 and 2013. It is not truly a "single payer" system, but it has created a central State government entity or "health care exchange" that oversees the health care for all Massachusetts residents. This Government agency also provides health care, guidelines and subsidies for those residents that are disabled, handicapped or poor. Because Mitt Romney was the governor of Massachusetts at the time the law was introduced it was nicknamed "*Romneycare*", and it is said that it is the model for "*ObamaCare*" (Affordable Health Care Act). We have already established that the population of the USA is 321 million. The population of Massachusetts in 2015 is just under 7 million. As a recipient of MassHealth I can attest that generally it works quite well, particularly for the disabled, handicapped and poor. However, to try and make a plan that works for 7 million people work for 321 million people is pure folly.

I do believe in theory that a "single payer" system is the morally correct approach to caring for the health of the population of any community. In my case, and I believe in most other peoples cases, our vagaries of health are largely the result of an unhealthy and dangerous environment, ignorance, poor diet or residing within a society that does not adhere to healthy activities. In my case the society in which I resided made possible an environment in which the Polio virus could be created and propagated. Although through ignorance, the society allowed an environment to be formed whereby certain innocent individuals became victims of this ignorance and reaped the results of society's slow attention to repairing the wrongs it had allowed to happen and replace the ignorance with enlightened knowledge and skills.

I think all Americans will agree that prior to "Obama Care" (Affordable Health Care Act) the Health Care system for America was either completely broken or at least in trouble. I think that those same Americans will agree that even with the best will in the world they could not say that "Obama Care" made the situation better but, in fact, made it worse.

In order to really understand why the "Health Care Industry" is in trouble it is necessary to look at the basic premise of the Industry. At the head of the "Health Care Industry" are the Insurance Companies. These companies are by definition "For Profit" companies. My studies in business have always taught me that "For Profit" companies are always most successful when they produce a "Product". They are not so successful when they try to provide a "service". For example when a "for profit" company tries to run a Railroad/Railway, a bus service or any kind of business that require profits but does not produce a "product", disaster usually follows an initial success and over time the service suffers in efficiency and quality. Fast-food restaurants are only successful when they produce a product – Hamburger, coffee, ice cream etc. Their service is of lesser importance than the actual product purchased. Their patrons patronize their establishments for the specialized products and not for the service they receive. The only time a "for profit" company is successful without a particular product associated with the company is when a service is offered that requires specialized capitalized equipment or the service offered requires a specialized skill or talent on the part of the owner of the company.

The "Health Care Industry" is a profit oriented industry and parts of it do have a "Product" based mandate. Most of the industry, however, is geared to the service of "Health Care" to its consumers. "Health Care" legislation that changes the basic mandate upon which "Health Care" in America is based creates as significant problem for the legislators. It is doubtful to my mind that this can be achieved any time soon. Furthermore the *"Preventative Health Care"* approach to "Health Care" is so entrenched in the American "Health Care" system that it is unlikely that the voters will accept its demise and replacement. The Insurance companies will not give up their strangle-hold on a very lucrative industry and their bean-counters that determine the *"Preventative Health Care"* policies will be reassigned to other duties or fired, but in either case they will not be providing the "statistics" that drive the *"Preventative Health Care"* system.

In other words if American "Health Care" is able to change its mandate to the "single payer" format this will increase the withdrawals from the workers paycheck, over time reduce the service quality we receive, but at the same time remove the Insurance companies hold over the industry. The "Health Care Industry" will have been "Nationalized" and this act will open the door for further industries being "Nationalized" and the USA will be well on the way to becoming a formal Socialist/Communist Country.

Although morally and ethically I personally believe that the "single payer" method is the right plan, I also realize that it took the UK 100 years to come anywhere close to a workable system, and after another 100 years the system still has some significant problems. Also with the process of change came the morphing to a socialist style of government and the concept of a Welfare State whereby the government obtained control of every aspect of everyone's individual lives.

It appears to me that if we are to *"secure the Blessings of Liberty to ourselves and our Posterity"* as indicated in the Constitution's Preamble, we should be aware of the consequences of the decisions we make today on the generations to come.


Respectfully Submitted

Kerry R. Scott

# "Health Care Industry

## vs.

# Health Care Service"

by

Kerry R. Scott

06/27/2017

I have been astounded as I have followed the various comments and opinions voiced by politicians, pundits and commentators, at the very limited and narrow nature of the comments on the various health care bills that have been presented. Without doubt almost all commentary is centered around making affordable health care available to all, providing health insurance care premiums within the reach of most Americans and confirming, albeit obliquely, a fulsome profit margin for the Insurance Companies. Very little, if any, commentary has come to my attention that describes these health care bills in terms of the patient, the doctor or the health care professional. There have been, to my count, five different health care bills presented in the last few years. Initially there was *"Hillary Care"* which never made it from the "start gate". Then *The Affordable Care Act* (otherwise known as *"Obama Care"*) was presented which became the "law of the Land" but needed to be "passed in order to find out what was in…" the bill. The next bill was presented, with the President's support, but withdrawn as the votes necessary to pass the bill were not available. The House of Representatives did pass a new bill called *The American Health Care* bill but the Senate would not accept it and decided to create their own bill, which at present is still in the throes of acrimonious discussion and as of the date of this essay has a delayed vote.

The question arises in my mind – why, with all the knowledge and experience available to our legislators – has it taken five bills and over eight years to come up with a viable plan – and why is Congress still floundering around trying to come up with a reasonable health care plan which will be of benefit to the patient?

The answer to this question is really the basis of this essay, in which I will propose a theory as why at the present time it will be impossible for Congress to come up with a successful plan to adequately cater to the Health Care needs of the American population and, in fact, should not even try to pass such a comprehensive configuration for society's collective health.

In discussing the latest attempt at a "Health Care Plan" I cannot help but start with the insurance companies. It is these insurance companies that, in fact, will control the financial aspect of any plan Congress contemplates. All insurance companies work on the basis of "probability". If where one resides has a high burglary crime rate and you have content insurance on the contents of your house, your content insurance premium will be higher than someone else that lives in a lesser crime area. If the above "Probability Scenario" can be attached to any situation it is likely to be of interest to an insurance company.

There are a number of logical rubrics for any insurance company to make a profit (their primary interest), they are as follows:

- The insurance companies work on the "Probability" that they will receive greater amount in premiums on any given insurance policy than they will pay out in benefits. Insurance companies "pay out less than they take in"
- The insurance company will charge premium amounts that guarantee the payout of benefits, provide a significant profit margin, and cover overheads and payroll.
- The basis of insurance companies "Probability" determination is that of statistics collected over a period of time and under particular conditions.
- "Probability" is determined by "probability algorithms" that use the raw statistics as a basis and provide a "risk" quotient otherwise known as actuarial tables.
- "Risk" is integral part of the insurance companies mandate – but only as "Controlled Risk".
- Generally the greater the "risk" the greater the cost – both to the insurance company and to the insured.
- Insurance companies are "for-profit" corporations and therefore their first and primary mandate is to provide a profit and dividends for their investors.

Taking all the above points into account and trying to apply them to Health Care legislation, a number of points become abundantly clear.

- To apply the statistics gathered from a sampling of individuals in particular age groups to 321 million people (the population of the USA) renders a "Probability" that the outcome will be accurate as nil.
- The Health Care of an individual is a personal matter and should not be controlled by a for-profit corporation.
- The "risk" one takes with regard to one's health is also a personal matter and again should not be controlled by funds, or a for-profit corporation.
- Health Care professionals should not have the care they can offer be controlled by a for-profit corporation based on a "risk" factor determined by the same For-profit Corporation.
- For the insurance company the diagnosis of illness or disability is a matter of statistics whereas for the health care professional it is a matter of knowledge and qualification, medical experience, observation and knowledge of the individual.

- "Preventative Care" is most important to the insurance company as it provides further detailed data as well as guaranteeing the necessity of constant visits to the medical professional for test and procedures whether needed or not. The driving force being the statistics being provided by the epidemiologists.
- Efficiency is the key ingredient in insurance company run Health Care. The greater number of patients a Health Care professional sees the greater number of premiums received and thus the greater the return to the investors. In insurance company run Health Care "Patient quotas" are necessary even thou no patient is the same and no patient is seeing the health care professional necessarily for the same reason.

From the foregoing it can be seen that the insurance companies view Health Care as an Industry – according to the insurance companies it must be an industry because it has a "market", investors and a corporate infrastructure. This "Industry" pays dividends to its investors and provides a reasonable (or perhaps an unreasonable) return for the investor's money. It treats the process of insurance the same way as it would, for example, car or house insurance. When a claim is made the insurance company processes it the same way it would a claim on any other kind of insurance policy. It asks the following questions:

- Is the claim covered under the policy?
- Is the claim amount within the guidelines set up by the company's Actuaries?
- How many other claims has this client made?
- What is the prognosis for further claims by this client?

Note that the holder of the policy is a client and is not considered a "Patient". That the "Patient" may be suffering from a disease or is handicapped or disabled is not a pertinent to the insurance company—they are simply interested in "business as usual"—pay the claim or refuse it! The insurance companies have no compassion for, or understanding of, the individual "Patient" but rather a "one-size-fits-all" approach thus safeguarding the "bottom line". This is not really as cynical as it sounds – this writer believes in the capitalistic approach – but not for some human issues and Health Care is one such issue. When a patient visits the doctor, to paraphrase a vernacular saying, "he/she is, what he/she is". In other words if the "Patient" is ill or has a "pre-existing condition" that is the condition that the doctor must address. The doctor is trained, experienced and qualified to be a professional to handle what appears before him or her. The terms of the Hippocratic Oath alone does not allow the doctor to turn away patients because they have a pre-existing condition or require treatment that is not covered by an insurance policy. This does happen, however, and when it does it is a prime example of "financial discrimination" – that is the poor are being discriminated against, not by the doctors (although if they go along with this policy they are complicit in the action and are therefore "co-conspirators") but by the insurance companies.

There is a huge conflict between the business approach and the human approach to Health Care. At present (and since the 1990's and *Hillary Care*) Congress seems determined that the People's

Health Care is a business issue – they keep referring to "Health Care" as an "Industry". The insurance company lobby is mighty strong and I believe what is going on is a war between those advocates of the humanistic approach to Health Care and the other side – the business approach to Health Care. Congress and the President are trying to forge a compromise between the two, and like previous presidents and congresses, they are failing. I believe that both sides of the issue certainly have some merit but intrinsically the "Humanistic" and "Business" approach for Health Care is mutually exclusive. A number of politicians have indicated that the issue is "complicated" it is not, it is "impossible"!

There is a simple solution to the stalemate in which Congress is at present wallowing. This solution, however, requires the outside insertion of the "People of America". It requires that the American people collectively decide that their Health Care is either an "Entitlement" or not. At present I do not believe that American society can collectively agree on this issue. (It should be pointed out that I am using the word "*Entitlement*" [capitalized] as a Noun in the contemporary format equaling a "*right of the people*" or "*required provision of the government by the people*".)

During the recent discussion on the latest Health Care legislation I have observed both Republican and Democrat Representatives and Senators indicate both sides of this issue; therefore initially we have to come to some conclusion as to the status of the concept of "Health Care for All".

In my previous essay on this subject --"*Third Time Lucky and Three Strikes and You Are Out*" (dated- 04/28/2017) I argued that the Constitution was vague concerning the "*welfare*" of the people – leaving the concept of the "*people's welfare*" to the discretion of Congress and that there was a possible difference between the "*welfare*" of the people and the "*welfare*" of the country. Health Care is obviously a sub-set or part of the "*welfare of the people*" and consequently, simply based on the Constitution it seems that legislation concerning the health care for the people is at the discretion of Congress. However for twenty three years and five massive legislation attempts neither Congress nor the People can agree upon a plan for Health Care.

It is necessary, therefore, to look beyond the Constitution and delve into the annals of history to find a real answer to whether or not the People are entitled to health care as a "*right*".

The *Declaration of Independence*, the *Constitution* and the *Bill of Rights* were all based on the concept of "*Natural Law*". The Declaration of Independence in particular starts out with the words:

"*When in the Course of human events it becomes necessary for one people to dissolve the political bands which have connected them with another and to assume among the powers of the earth, the separate and equal station to which the Laws of Nature and of Nature's God entitle them, a decent respect to the opinions of mankind requires that they should declare the causes which impel them to the separation.*"

This paragraph indicates that although the people are *"separate"* from others, they *"assume"* an *"equal station"* to which *"the Laws of Nature and of Nature's God entitle them...."* So what are these *"Laws of Nature"* or *"Natural Law"* that make us all *"separate and equal"*? It is here that this writer recalls the saying *"fools rush in where angels fear to tread"*. I am not a legal scholar and by no means an expert in any kind of law, let alone "natural Law", I do, however, pride myself as a reasoning person and one with a modicum of common sense and so it is with some trepidation and apologies for mistakes in interpretation, that I venture forth into the murky and convoluted world of the interpretation of "Natural Law".

For some, "Natural Law" is a philosophy that provides to us certain rights that come from nature. These rights are made available to us simply because we are human, further we can understand those rights through human reason. It was on this basis that Thomas Jefferson oversaw the writing of the Declaration of Independence and in particular crafted the opening sentence (seen above) to include the reference to the *"Laws of Nature"* and of *"Nature's God"*. It has been generally accepted that the inclusion of the "Laws of Nature" and the reference to "God" indicates that the crafters of the Declaration wanted to emphasize that there was a higher power above either of the separated parties *i.e.* The American Colonies and Britain as well as any human laws that were crafted.

The second paragraph of the *Declaration Of Independence* reads thusly:

*"We hold these truths to be self-evident, that all men are created equal, that they are endowed by their Creator with certain unalienable Rights, that among these are Life, Liberty and the pursuit of Happiness."*

From the above it can be seen that the *Declaration Of Independence* in two paragraphs moves from *"Natural Law"* to *"Human Rights"* and that *"Life, Liberty and the pursuit of Happiness"* are only *"among"* those *"unalienable rights"* the People may enjoy.

Thomas Jefferson referenced his ideas on "Natural Law" from both John Locke and Thomas Paine who also used the word *"unalienable"* to describe *"Human Rights"*. Thomas Paine in *"The Rights of Man"* wrote that these natural rights include *"all the intellectual rights, or rights of the mind and also those rights of acting as an individual for his own comfort and happiness, which are not injurious to the natural rights of others."*

I think that Judge Andrew P. Napolitano sums up the situation best in his book *"The Constitution in Exile"* where he indicates:

*The significance of the Declaration [of Independence]....is that it is believed to contain the philosophical underpinnings of the Constitution. In other words, an understanding of Natural Law, its conferral of rights upon men and women, and the relationship between those rights and the role of government is fundamental to understand and interpret the Constitution properly"*

At this stage it is, perhaps, a good idea to revisit the description of "Natural Laws" given above:

*"Natural Law" is a philosophy that provides to us certain rights that come from nature.*

It is important to note the word "Philosophy" as it is to note the words of Judge Napolitano when he states, *"that [the Declaration of Independence] is believed to contain the philosophical underpinnings of the Constitution"*. Again note the word *"philosophical"*. The arguments for "Natural Law" in this instance are more philosophical than they are legislative. This is because they stem from Christianity particularly referenced in Paul's Epistle to the Romans (Romans 2). There are, however, many other theories on "Natural Law" best summed up in the book "The Constitution of Liberty" by F. A. Hayek where in Chapter 16, *The Decline of the Law"* he indicates:

*".....we have not explicitly considered.... [t]he conception of a law of nature, which to many still offers the answer to our most important questions. We have... ...avoided discussing... [issues] with reference to this conception because the numerous schools which go under this name hold really different theories... What all the schools of natural law agree upon is the existence of rules which are not of the deliberate making of any lawgiver [legislator]. They agree that all positive law derives its validity from some rules that have not in this sense been made by men but which can be "found" and that these rules provide both the criterion for the justice of positive law and the ground for men's obedience to it."*

Mr. Hayek brings a new term to the essay, that of *"positive law"*. Positive laws are laws made by a Legislature; they are human made laws as opposed to Natural laws that stem from Nature. The Declaration of Independence, as already indicated is more of a Philosophical document than it is a legislative document. It lays the philosophical ground work for the Constitution that, as it was legislated is an example of *"positive law"*.

There are now two distinct types of "rights". Natural law comprises inherent rights provided by "God, Nature or reason" and Positive law that are human-made laws that specify an action or the establishment of specific rights.

It is the conflict between suggesting that the People's Health Care is in the area of Natural Law or can be handled within the area of Positive Law that is creating the stale-mate in solving this issue. At present the Congress is treating Peoples Health Care as a Positive Law issue, however as such, the legislature is targeting the cost and format of implementing the system rather than concentrating on the service that should be provided to the patient. **Furthermore this conflict is also a result of the collective American Society not being culturally evolved sufficiently to make the determination that the vulnerable in society should be helped and supported as, I believe, their rights under Natural Law dictate.**

As indicated previously in this essay – the Health Care of our society is part of the general welfare of the American People. In 1936 that the Supreme Court struck down a Federal spending program that was for the "general welfare of the Country" indicating that it invaded the States rights as indicated by the Tenth Amendment. At the same time the Supreme Court also managed to confuse the whole matter by determining that the concept of "general welfare" was left to the discretion of Congress.

If the collective American Society is going to rise to the occasion and make Health Care a "Natural Right" then, at the same time Heath Care should be treated as a component of a larger "Natural Right" the implementation of a "Welfare State": whereby the "vulnerable" of society (the poor, the sick, the unemployed, children and the elderly) are all protected and supported. However in order for a society to implement a "Welfare State" that same society should have a cultural identity which in turn requires that their country have a secure identity, status and longevity. In addition, the government of that country needs a strong mandate from the "People". The main component for a society to achieve a "Cultural Identity" is, however, "longevity". Society evolves, it does not suddenly become secure and established. This evolution takes time and thus for this essay the following sentence becomes almost a lynchpin in developing a theory on why Congress cannot seem to be able to pass an adequate Health Care bill.

**All societies evolve and develop at different rates and in different ways.**

America has had about 250 years during which the American society has obviously evolved significantly within the basis of the Constitution to determine "Positive Law" and the Declaration of Independence determining "Natural Law".

**I do not believe, however, that American Society is yet at the point that as a collective society they are able to mandate that either Health Care or the Welfare of the People of America can be considered a "Natural Law".**

In 1942 the Beveridge Report published, and British society recognized, five "Giant Evils" namely: squalor, ignorance, want, idleness and disease. This led to the implementation of a series of statutes that created the "Welfare State". Britain has been a "Welfare State" since that time regardless of the governing party and their policies. The creation of a "Welfare State" was a collective societal decision, founded on the principal of "Natural Law" and was intended to help and support the most vulnerable in the society. It was completely bi-partisan. Since 1944 there have been considerable tweaks to the system and severe criticisms as well as significant successes – but the underlying concept of helping those less fortunate than the majority has prevailed.

The formation of a *Welfare State*, however, took many hundreds of years to evolve. The earliest statute that could be considered any form of Welfare was in 1349 when King Edward III created an *Ordinance of Labourers* which froze wages and forced a competitive approach to hiring employees. The whole Ordinance, and the subsequent acts were in response to the outbreak of the Black Death in 1348 – 1350 which decimated the population killing between 30 –40% of the work force.

Starting in Tudor times the various statutes that concerned the poor became known as *"Poor Laws"* and this continued to be the nomenclature until the early 1900's. In 1495 King Henry VII Parliament passed the *Vagabonds and Beggars Act* but at this stage it must be pointed out that most of the statutes that were passed as *"Poor Laws"* were in reality more punitive than benevolent. In 1531 Henry VIII instituted by proclamation that beggars should be confined to one area in which to beg. This was the time of the *Reformation* and the dissolution of the monasteries. As it was the church and monasteries that produced most of the relief to the poor the demise of those necessary institutions meant much of this relief was lost. Elizabeth I was as punitive toward the poor as was her Tudor predecessors. Her *1575 Poor Act* required towns to provide raw materials on which the poor were to work and if they refused to work they were sent to houses of correction. This heralded the later creation of the Workhouse. The first complete code for *poor relief* was set up in the *Act for the Relief of the Poor* in 1597. It should be noted that this was the first time the word "relief" was used in a Statute with regard to the poor thus indicating, perhaps, the beginning of a more benign approach to the poor. The passing of this Statute coincided with a deteriorating economic climate caused by population growth as well as the increased availability of American Silver and thus, perhaps, the number of the "poor" increased considerably. In 1601 *The Elizabethan Poor Law* was formalized and condensed earlier practices of poor relief. Although not thought of at the time this was indeed a harsh treatment of the poor. This law became known as the *Old Poor Law* and was a Parish based system. The primary concern of this law was to deal with vagabonds and beggars and punishing them harshly if they did not make an effort to re-enter society – which in most cases, even if they wanted to, they could not achieve.

In 1696 Parliament founded the *Bristol Corporation of the Poor* which established a Workhouse in the city of Bristol for the benefit of the poor. This heralded the creation of many Workhouses in many towns and cities throughout Britain. Some were authorized by Parliament and some were simply set up by the various local authorities (Councils). The workhouses combined both work and living quarters for the poor but also acted as "houses of correction" for offenders guilty of "Petty Offences". In 1723 *The Workhouse Test Act* was passed that gave authority for the establishment of Parochial Workhouses to be set up by single parishes.

It is important to note that *The Workhouse Test Act* produced national attention to both the Workhouse program as well as indicating for the first time the poor was the responsibility of the community and although supported by the Government and (at the time) the Church, it was the *local* community that bore this responsibility. It cannot be said, however, that conditions within the Workhouse were adequate. Although they varied from one Workhouse to another, the conditions by any standard were considered atrocious. This was because, although, the poor was, by the middle of the Century, considered in a more benign way, their poor status was still considered their own fault and therefore a punitive approach was still extant – They deserved to exist in appalling conditions because they were poor. In addition the Workhouses were still constructed as "Houses of Correction" and still also housed "petty offenders".

In 1776, the year of the signing of the American Declaration of Independence, in Britain there were 1,912 parish workhouses housing almost 100,000 paupers and by the end of the Eighteenth Century it is estimated that a million were receiving some sort of poor relief.

*The Speenhamland System* (named after the town Speenhamland in Berkshire, England) was introduced in 1795 as an amendment to the *Elizabethan Poor Law*. This system, while locally administered, was based on the price of grain which at the time was high priced and in short supply (mainly because of Britain's involvements in the French Revolutionary and Napoleonic Wars). The main difference between this poor relief system and the ones that preceded it, however, was the fact that this system gave a "means test" prior to awarding the relief.

On page 7 of this essay I indicated that:

**All societies evolve and develop at different rates and in different ways.**

By 1795 Britain had experienced just less than Four Hundred years of social evolution with regard to those in society that were generally classed as "Vulnerable". After 400 years they had managed to develop a social system whereby they could begin to approach the "poor" issue in a less punitive manner, provide *poor relief* (albeit it minimal and considerably less than adequate) and had created a "*means test*" to determine the validity of awarding the "*relief*".

By 1787 America had declared Independence from Britain and had drafted the Constitution for America and it was ratified by the nine States. Obviously the priority at the time was the exploration of the newly formed country and the protection of that same country. The American Culture was in its very earliest stages of development and the concept of a society was beginning to emerge and be ready to develop and evolve.

Meanwhile, at the other side of the "pond" the evolution of the British Society is continuing. In 1782 Workhouses were created solely for the aged and infirm. Identifying, for the first time, different divisions of the "Vulnerable" in society and not just making the generic category of the "poor" and "Petty Offenders" In 1834 the *Poor Law Amendment Act* was passed. This in effect nationalized the Workhouses and programs for "poor relief". It created a *Poor Law Commission* to oversea the national operation of the system. It did nothing, however, to improve the conditions in the workhouses themselves nor help the plight of the poor wretches that were forced to inhabit those prison-like buildings. In 1846 conditions in the Andover Workhouse were determined as "*inhumane and dangerous*" and as a result the Government replaced the *Poor Law Commission* with a *Poor Law Board* thus making the government overseeing and administrating the Poor Law directly. In 1888 County Councils were formed and thus "*Public Housing*" was created, therefore making possible the catering to the "Vulnerable" of the Society outside of the "Poor Law" auspices. For various reasons, but primarily because of the creation of "*Public Housing*", the Poor Law system began to decline during the 1900's. A Royal Commission was set up in 1905 mandated to evaluate the "Poor Law" and look into what improvements could be made. The two conflicting reports were in essence ignored by the then Liberal Party government in order for the Government to introduce their own independent plan. This plan titled (for the first time) *"Welfare Legislation"* provided "Social Services", "Old age pensions" and "National Insurance" (Social Security). The term "Workhouse" was replaced by the term "Poor Law Institution" but gradually the whole concept of the Workhouse and the "Poor Law" system disappeared and was replaced by "Welfare Reform". In 1936 the "Poor Law Institutions" only catered for 13% of those of society that were receiving "Poor Relief". The 1942 Beveridge Report in conjunction with the 1909 minority report of the Royal Commission on the "Poor Law" recommended the creation of a "unified medical service" that comprised of "comprehensive health and rehabilitation services for prevention and cure of disease". It is interesting to note that this report created a "cross-party" (non-partisan) consensus to introduce a *National Health Service.* In 1948 the "Poor Law" system was finally abolished and the "National Health Service" became the law of the land.

In Britain the term "Welfare State" is a composite term which includes statutes on health, education, employment and Social Security. The creation of a "Welfare State" was not an idea originating at one time or with one person – no one invented the "Welfare State". The whole idea evolved as the Government and the Society of Britain evolved. It was only after about 600 years of development that the British Society could agree on the format and the way that the "vulnerable" of its society could be protected and helped. That is clearly demonstrated in 1948 with "cross-party" (non-partisan) consensus that passed the National Health Act. As can be clearly seen from the description above, the journey that Britain traveled in order to achieve a "Welfare State" included many missteps and digressions into "blind-alleys", there were casualties and adjustments to human priorities had to be made. Collective opinions had to be adjusted and bigotry needed to be addressed. The concept of Human dignity also had to be clarified and respected.

As I have indicated twice before in this essay:

**All societies evolve and develop at different rates and in different ways.**

And the journey of societal evolution that America takes will probably be different to that Britain took, but whatever journey America does take to protect and develop the vulnerable of their society will, by necessity, require "consensus" not only by the lawmakers but also the population as a whole. Population consensus will require society to have a common goal, a similar sense of purpose and a compassion for the less fortunate.

American has evolved considerably in the last 250 years and has achieved many parts that go toward creating a social environment that protects and develops the vulnerable of the society (Social Security, Public Housing, education etc.). 250 years is not enough time, however, for the evolution of 321 million people to come to a consensus. The governed, as one voice, needs to tell the Government how they want the "vulnerable" in the society protected and developed. The solutions Britain came up with might help but in the final analysis solutions that work for 64 million people in Britain most probably will not work for 321 million people in America. American society needs some time to evolve into an identifiable and overt Culture with an established consensus on national values and morality.

Finally, and combining all the above into one sentence, it is too soon to try and create a federal Health Care system – let the Tenth Amendment lead the way and for now let the individual States create whatever kind of Health Care system their constituents require. Congress, retreat gracefully, and go back to your States and wait until evolution has played its part and then "return to the fray".


Respectfully Submitted

Kerry R. Scott

# "Health Care Industry

# VS.

# Health Care Service"

by

Kerry R. Scott

## <u>Addendum I</u>

07/12/2017

Very quickly after the distribution of the essay "Health Care Industry VS. Health Care Service", the very tragic news report concerning the plight of Charlie Gard and his parents broke over here in the USA.

Charlie Gard is an eleven month old boy with a disease called mitochondrial DNA depletion syndrome. Charlie is said to be one of only 16 people to have ever had the condition and there appears that there is no treatment for the disease within the UK. Charlie is presently a patient at Great Ormond Street Hospital in London UK where Doctors believe that Charlie should be allowed to "die with dignity" and applied for permission to have his ventilator switched off. On April 11th 2017 the High Court in the UK gave permission to the hospital for Charlie's ventilator to be switched off against the pleas of the parents. On May 25th 2017 the Court of Appeals in the UK upheld the High Court Ruling. The ventilator was scheduled to be turned off on May 31st 2017 but Britain's Supreme Court agreed to review the case, and the hospital delayed the termination until the Supreme Court had made a decision. At the June 8th 2017 hearing the Supreme Court upheld the decision to switch Charlie's life support off. The parents then took their case to the European Court of Human Rights but on June 27th 2017 the court indicated that they would not intervene. Charlie's life-support was, therefore, expected to be switched off on Friday June 30. After a plea from Charlie's parents Great Ormond Street Hospital agreed to grant them more time with little Charlie to say goodbye. At the date of this essay, Charlie's fate is still in flux. Both Pope Francis and President Trump have offered help. A New York hospital with significant experience in dealing with Charlie's disease (albeit still experimental) has offered to treat Charlie. The United States Congress is voting to award Charlie Gard American citizenship and the parent's of Charlie have raised over 1.3 million pounds to pay for Charlie's treatment and transportation to the USA. The parents have been given a very short amount of time to prove that moving Charlie for treatment to the USA will improve Charlie's condition and be productive.

I have had a number of responses concerning my essay, some of which seem to represent that the writers thought I was in favor of a National Health System. To be clear; I am in favor of the "vulnerable" of society being looked after by the society in which they reside. I define the "vulnerable" as:

- The Disabled.
- The Ill, infirm or sick.
- The Developmentally Delayed
- Children
- The Elderly
- The Poor
- The unemployed

Whether those "vulnerable" wish to be "looked after" and whether this requires a National Health System is the individual's final and binding decision and not a decision that can be made for them by society. The disposition of an individual's Health is a "Natural Law" as defined by being determined by "God, Nature or Reason". I believe that as a "Natural Law" or a "Natural Right" this right cannot and should not be overridden by "positive law". Whether this position requires a National Health Care system or not depends on the way in which a society evolves and the political position of the Government when the People decide that the protection of the "vulnerable" should be the responsibility of Society. However this decision does not obviate the individual's right to decide for themselves the right of survival.

On another but related point I was horrified by Angela Merkel's opening remarks at the G20 Summit. I realize, of course, that the summit is only concerned with world financial issues, but what caused me real concern was her assumption that her apparent "ideal" (and one supposes Germany in general) was a system of government that could only be described as "Global Communism".

Another perhaps, off point observation that I have made in the last couple weeks is the loose use of the following terms: Liberal, Communist, Socialist, Ultra-left, Progressive, The Progressive Left, Left Winger, Libertarian, Conservative, Right Winger, Ultra-right. It should be noted that I have left out the titles of "Democrat", "Independent" and "Republican"; this is because I use these terms simply to indicate the party to which a particular individual may belong rather than the political ideals he or she may espouse.

I think one of the reasons as to the confusion some of my readers may have concerning my support of a National Health Care system is a lack of definition of the political labels used with respect in the ideology associated with a particular label. In order to make clear the different ideals in play with particular labels I am going to start with dividing the political spectrum in two. On the left are Liberals and on the Right are Conservatives. Those individuals that have some ideals in both the Conservative camp as well as the Liberal Camp are labeled as

"Centralists". Recently I was interested to witness a description of a "true progressive". I am paraphrasing but in essence according to this individual:

'A "true progressive" is a person who believes that the Human is in control of all aspects of his or her life, believes that Government has the answer to all issues and is the ultimate authority, whether elected or not, on all matters. The "true progressive" also believes that there is no higher power than the human and humans are as a consequence responsible for all positive and negative aspect of our existence and environment. A "true progressive" believes that only "Positive Law" is relevant to the human and therefore does not acknowledge the existence of "Natural Law" by "God, Nature or Reason"'.

On the other hand, I suppose a "true conservative" is a person who believes in the total liberty of the individual, minimal government and the individual's "pursuit of happiness" while enjoying their "inalienable rights". A "true conservative is also a believer in the "capitalistic system" whereby they are in control of their own destiny and are responsible for their own perceived success or failure. What a "true conservative" achieves and owns belongs to themselves and they are not obligated to be responsible nor contribute to society as a whole.

The political spectrum is really a continuum from the "true progressive" on the left indicated above to the opposite side of the spectrum the "true conservative" on the right. The examples and descriptions seen above are extreme examples of these political positions. The other labels fall somewhere between the two and depending on the individual's interpretation of the label depends where they fall on this continuum.

Applying the above points to the evolution of society indicates that the Natural Laws must remain intact even if society evolves to the point that puts the Natural Laws in jeopardy. There is a fine metaphorical line that exists between an "evolving society", whereby the Natural Laws are maintained and a "devolving society" whereby the natural laws are replaced by "positive law" control. In the Charlie Gard situation Natural Law indicates that the parents have the ultimate decision making power over their son. When the courts determined that he should remain in the hospital and die a "dignified death" they relied on a positive law; giving precedence to the National Health System over the parental Natural Law of responsibility. In the process the courts defied Natural Law. The courts allowed the system of an evolved society to take control of a situation that should be controlled by the individual. Further they placed the human (positive law) above that of "God, Nature or Reason" (Natural Law). The English Courts and European Union Court of Human Rights practiced "bad" positive law. An American court could not (and one hopes would not!) have made such a ruling as it would be in conflict with our "unalienable rights" as indicated in the Declaration of Independence. With this court ruling I believe the British Society is now "devolving" rather than "evolving".

I have Just learned that the court has given the parents of Charlie Gard two days to prove to the court that further treatment in the USA would provide improvement in Charlie's condition otherwise the court will substantiate the ruling that the hospital should take Charlie off the life support system. This to me seems the most evil ruling I have ever heard. This contravenes the Natural Law of parental responsibility for their children's well being and represents state assisted murder. This is quite clearly a "eugenics" ruling and represents that the European Union is well on the way towards a "New Holocaust" whereby the "vulnerable" of society become its victims. The National Health System of the UK appears to make decisions concerning the health of an individual based on "bad" positive law which includes laws (most probably under misleading titles) under the concept of Eugenic philosophy. The "vulnerable" of society need the *protection of society* not to be *eradicated by society* officials that purport to perform the protection but in reality respond to the situational ethics of the time.

This horrific situation coupled with Angela Merkel's comments indicated previously in this essay, seem eerily similar to Germany's build up toward the Second World War. Are we looking toward the European Union, led by Germany trying once again to create a "Reich"? The "Fourth Reich"! The German word "Reich" is literally translated meaning "realm" but in the German vernacular is has a more of a connotation toward that of an "Empire" and control. The translation of NAZI Party is "The National Socialist German Workers' Party". Taking Angel Merkel's comments and the European Union's court's ruling into account is seems that we are dangerously close to an evangelical "true progressive" approach to a Europe with aspirations of global control. Mikhail Gorbachev said it best when he indicated the following:

> *"The most puzzling development in politics during the last decade is the apparent determination of Western European leaders to re-create the Soviet Union in Western Europe."*

It seems that ignoring "Natural Law" leads us all down a path whereby Truth is relative to the context in which we find ourselves and our freedoms are negotiated away to be replaced by control from the unelected elite. The phrase "security from cradle to the grave" should now be changed to "control from cradle to the grave".

Although I have used this quote before I can think of no better way than to close this addendum with these wise words from Winston Churchill:

> *"Socialism is a philosophy of failure, the creed of ignorance, and the gospel of envy, its inherent virtue is the equal sharing of misery."*
> Winston Churchill

Respectfully Submitted

Kerry R. Scott

# "Health Care Industry

## vs.

# Health Care Service"

by

Kerry R. Scott

## <u>Addendum II</u>

*A Baby and an Elder Senator with Catastrophic Illnesses.*

07/25/2017


I am not usually shocked or awed by a week's happenings either in the political arena or changes in USA Foreign policy, but last week was the exception. Everything in which I was interested or in which I was personally involved seemed to be directly linked to some aspect of Health Care. The ramifications and personal and general impact of the health care events and the individual liberties that the events compromised horrified me. I came to America (Legally!) because I believed in, among other liberties, the Freedom of Speech and particularly the personal freedom to control my own life. Western Culture seems to be hurtling toward the evil concept of Socialism and last week I saw three issues that pointed that the rate upon which we were moving was increasing. I have related in this Addendum these three issues and pointed out how they impact, in this case, our individual health care.

**The Health Care Provider**

A short while ago it appeared that I needed my cholesterol medication prescription renewed. My pharmacy kindly contacted my doctor for authorization to renew the "script" and thus started a bureaucratic nightmare that cost the American taxpayer a serious amount of money. I should explain that because I am a polio survivor and suffer from Post Polio Syndrome I am enrolled in Medicare and MassHealth (Medicaid). As a partial result of Post Polio Syndrome I also suffer from high Blood Pressure and increased Cholesterol levels (both of which are under control with the use of medication). I have taken the Cholesterol medication for some years and have the prescription renewed on a three month basis. I requested my refill of the prescription by telephone to my pharmacy and was informed that I should wait an extra day as the prescription had expired and the health care provider needed to renew the script. Two hours later I received a telephone call from the Pharmacy indicating that my request had been denied by the health care professional with no reason given except to indicate that I should call my primary care physician for further information. I put through a telephone call to my primary care physician and spoke initially to the receptionist and then was put through to my doctor's nurse. She explained that it was "Practice policy" to require the doctor's patients that were on cholesterol medication to visit the practice every six months to have their blood pressure taken and for a "medication review".

She further pointed out that the medication prescription could not be renewed unless I came in for an appointment. In short they were holding my medication "hostage" in order for me to attend an appointment. I pointed out that I had an appointment scheduled in early December, that I was in a wheel chair and that I took my blood pressure every day myself with a blood pressure machine that was calibrated to the Practice's blood pressure equipment. I also pointed out that it was very difficult for me to make the visit to the practice as I had to organize transportation via a wheelchair van to and from the practice that was over 10 miles away from my home. This made no difference to the nurse and she repeated ad nauseam that it was "Practice Policy". I must say the conversation became rather acrimonious as I felt that I was being looked upon as simply a subject of "Practice Policy" rather than a "patient" with a particular set of circumstances that made my call to the practice necessary. I ended up terminating the call abruptly and after calming down I called back to make this "hallowed" appointment. On this call I talked with the receptionist and she was more rational and I managed to make the appointment for the next week. In the process I found out that this appointment was scheduled to last just 15 minutes – as is the same for any other patient coming in for their six month monitor appointment.

It should be pointed out that if you are a recipient of benefits from Medicare and MassHealth (Medicare) and you are wheelchair bound without transportation, transportation is provided for you at no charge to and from medical appointments. A "PT—1" form is provided to a transportation state agency indicating the source and destination of the trip by the medical health provider. The state agency then puts the trip out for bids and the winner of the bid is then authorized to pick the patient up and return him back home after the appointment.

In my case my "PT—1" form was nearly expired and so before I could schedule the transportation I had to make sure that the date was cleared for transportation to and from the appointment. When this was accomplished I contacted the transportation state agency to schedule the appointment. Usually this requires a telephone call with being put on hold for over an hour but in this case I was lucky as I was on hold for only 45 minutes.

My appointment was scheduled for a Monday, and the Thursday before the lucky transportation company that had successfully bid on my "job" contacted me by telephone and confirmed that I was actually going to the appointment and that I needed a wheelchair van. At the same time they indicated their name and telephone number.

Unfortunately I recognized both the name of the company as well as the telephone number. This was the same company that had taken me to an appointment a year ago and, as the doctor was running 10 minutes late he had left to take another job and did not return. I was left in a power chair without a cell phone no water or food in the middle of an Industrial Park. The transportation agency when called indicated that someone would take me back home but they did not know when this would happen. My appointment ended at 10:00 a.m., at 4:00 p.m. when still no one had returned to pick me up I made other arrangements for both the chair and myself. I managed to arrive home at 5:30.p.m. At 6:30 p.m. the transportation company telephoned to indicate that they were at the industrial park to pick me up and where was I? The driver seemed most put-out that I had not waited the eight and half hours for him to return.

On the day of the appointment the Chair Car arrived on time and I was pleased to observe that the driver was not the same driver that left me high-and-dry the year before. My appointment was scheduled for 10:15.a.m. and we arrived in time for the appointment. I indicated to the driver that I was concerned to know whether he was waiting for me or was coming back at 11:15 a.m. when I booked the Chair-car for my return journey. The driver checked by telephone to his "boss" and indicated to me that he had permission to wait for the conclusion of my appointment. I checked in with the receptionist and was quickly called by the nurse assistant. I had pre-prepared a typed list of all my medications as well as a report on my blood pressure for the previous two weeks. The nurse assistant took my blood pressure checked the list of medications I had prepared and then left and indicated that the nurse practitioner would be with me shortly. She arrived shortly after and checked my breathing. She indicated that they would be renewing the cholestcrol medication. She indicated that the appointment was ending and I returned to the waiting room and the waiting chair-car. I arrived at the doctor's office at approximately 10:10.a.m. and was back in the Chair Car at approximately 10:40.a.m. I remind the reader that I am under Medicare and MassHealth (Medicaid). The personnel necessary for my less than necessary (but determined by Practice Protocol) appointment was:

At the doctor's office:

- A Nurse Practitioner
- A Nurse Assistant
- A Practice Receptionist

At the Transportation state agency:

- A Transportation Scheduler
- The bidding coordinator
- The Bidding contractor

At the Transportation Company:

- The Chair Car Driver
- The Dispatcher
- The Supervisor/owner

The above is a prime example of why the American Health Care system (i.e. Obama Care) is in chaos. In my case the reason for the appointment is with regard to an arbitrary office protocol rather than a medical necessity. My particular medical situation did not fit neatly into the Practice's medical protocol and there was not provision for the practice to adjust the protocol to fit a particular patient's requirements. A one-size-fits-all approach cannot be made to be effective in Health Care where each patient is an individual needing individual attention. That is why Health Care should not be an INDUSTRY but a SERVICE. Seeing a patient every six months may be a fine policy for some or even most patients that are taking cholesterol medication, but not necessarily all patients need this especially if they find attending the doctor's office a daunting and difficult task. If my doctor and I had had a discussion and came to the mutual conclusion that because of some individual medical reason I should schedule an appointment every six months then that would be logical and rational, but to simply make an arbitrary office protocol applicable to all patients within a certain group to schedule such appointments is socialized medicine at its worst. Moreover it takes the control of one's health care away from the individual and places it in the hands of the health agency and then ultimately to the State (i.e. Government). As I move onto the next item in the weeks evil Health Care activities it can be seen how the removal of the individuals control over small aspects of one's own health care can lead to catastrophically evil determinations of life and death.

**The Hospital and Court**

My appointment was scheduled for the Monday of last week, on the Tuesday we learned that Charlie Gard had passed away. In addendum I, I covered Charlie's tragic story and his parent efforts to allow for his survival and the possible improvement of his condition. I am going to quote the parents complete statement of saying good bye to Charlie and then I am going to comment.

The statement reads as follows and is striking in what it reveals about Charlie's case:

*"Firstly, I would like to thank our legal team who have worked tirelessly on our behalf for free. And to the nurses and staff at Great Ormond Street Hospital who have cared for Charlie and kept him comfortable and stable for so long.*

*We would also like to thank everybody who supported us, including all the people here for us today. This is one of the hardest things that we will ever have to say and we are about to do the hardest thing that we'll ever have to do, which is to let our beautiful little Charlie go.*

*Put simply, this is about a sweet, gorgeous innocent little boy who was born with a rare disease who had a real genuine chance at life and a family who loved him so very dearly. And that's why we fought so hard for him. We are truly devastated to say that following the most recent MRI scan of Charlie's muscles as requested in a recent MDT meeting by Dr Hirano.*

*As Charlie's devoted and loving parents, we've decided that it is no longer in Charlie's best interest to pursue treatment and we will let our son go and be with the angels.*

*The American and Italian team were still willing to treat Charlie after seeing his recent MRI and EEG perform last week, but there is one simple reason why treatment cannot now go ahead and that is time. A whole lot of time has been wasted. We are now in July and our poor boy has been left to just lie in hospital for months without any treatment whilst lengthy court battles have been fought. Tragically having had Charlie's medical notes reviewed by independent experts, we now know had Charlie been given the treatment sooner, he would have had the potential to be a normal healthy little boy.*

*Despite his condition in January, Charlie's muscles were in pretty good shape and far from showing irreversible catastrophic structural brain damage. Dr Hirano and other experts say his brain scans and EEGs were those of a relatively normal child of his age. We knew that ourselves because as his parents, we knew our son, which is why we continued fighting.*

*Charlie's been left for his illness to deteriorate devastatingly to the point of no return.*

*This has also never been about 'parents know best'.*

*All we wanted to do was take Charlie from one world-renowned hospital to another world-renowned hospital in the attempt to save his life and to be treated by the world leader in mitochondrial disease. We'll have to live with the what-ifs, which will haunt us for the rest of our lives.*

*Despite the way that our beautiful son has been spoken about sometimes, as if he is not worthy of a chance at life, our son is an absolute warrior and we could not be prouder of him and we will miss him terribly.*

*His body, heart and soul may soon be gone, but his spirit will live on for eternity and he will make a difference to people's lives for years to come. We will make sure of that.*

*We are now going to spend our last precious moments with our son Charlie who unfortunately won't make his first birthday in just under two weeks' time.*

*And we will ask that our privacy is respected during this very difficult time.*

*To Charlie we say mummy and daddy, we love you so much. We always have and we always will and we are so sorry we couldn't save you.*

*Sweet dreams baby, sleep tight our beautiful little boy. We love you!"*

Although I have indicated before that Health Care system in the USA is inevitably leading us to a "single Payer" system (i.e. a National Health system of Government control), and the evolution of society should lead us to a position whereby the "vulnerable" of society are "looked after", Charlie Gard's situation is without doubt a National System of Health Care going "rogue". Whether a Health Care system is an "Industry" or a "service" (i.e. profit making or "non-profit"), the natural law of parents have the responsibility of their children's well being should not be compromised. The institution administrating any health care system (either an Industry or a Service) does not have the right or responsibility to make "life or death" decisions that naturally by "Nature, God or Reason" belong to the parents. But what is significantly egregious in Charlie Gard's situation is that had the hospital and the courts not been so arrogantly stubborn that their policy was in the best interest of their patient in January 2017, according to the doctor called in to evaluate Charlie, he had the significant *potential to be a normal healthy little boy*.

*" Had* [he] *been given the treatment sooner"* claims the Doctor and Charlie's Father, Charlie might have lived and what is more, could have grown up to be a productive and thankful member of society. Instead the courts and hospital have left in their evil wake distraught and possible bitter parents and have possibility deprived society of potentially productive and beautiful human being. Although both the courts and the hospital have dismissed the claim, this was indeed a "Eugenics" act and is an apparent example of "State-assisted Murder". I am ashamed to be English and if I could I would renounce my citizenship of the UK forthwith. I am so pleased that I no longer live in that blighted and God-forsaken country where the government has the power of life and death over individuals and even innocent babies.

**The Government and the Senate.**

On 07/25/2017 Senator McCain made the following speech to the members of the Senate:

*"Mr. President:*

*"I've stood in this place many times and addressed as president many presiding officers. I have been so addressed when I have sat in that chair, as close as I will ever be to a presidency.*

*"It is an honorific we're almost indifferent to, isn't it. In truth, presiding over the Senate can be a nuisance, a bit of a ceremonial bore, and it is usually relegated to the more junior members of the majority.*

*"But as I stand here today – looking a little worse for wear I'm sure – I have a refreshed appreciation for the protocols and customs of this body, and for the other ninety-nine privileged souls who have been elected to this Senate.*

*"I have been a member of the United States Senate for thirty years. I had another long, if not as long, career before I arrived here, another profession that was profoundly rewarding, and in which I had experiences and friendships that I revere. But make no mistake, my service here is the most important job I have had in my life. And I am so grateful to the people of Arizona for the privilege – for the honor – of serving here and the opportunities it gives me to play a small role in the history of the country I love.*

*"I've known and admired men and women in the Senate who played much more than a small role in our history, true statesmen, giants of American politics. They came from both parties, and from various backgrounds. Their ambitions were frequently in conflict. They held different views on the issues of the day. And they often had very serious disagreements about how best to serve the national interest.*

*"But they knew that however sharp and heartfelt their disputes, however keen their ambitions, they had an obligation to work collaboratively to ensure the Senate discharged its constitutional responsibilities effectively. Our responsibilities are important, vitally important, to the continued success of our Republic. And our arcane rules and customs are deliberately intended to require broad cooperation to function well at all. The most revered members of this institution accepted the necessity of compromise in order to make incremental progress on solving America's problems and to defend her from her adversaries.*

*"That principled mindset, and the service of our predecessors who possessed it, come to mind when I hear the Senate referred to as the world's greatest deliberative body. I'm not sure we can claim that distinction with a straight face today.*

*"I'm sure it wasn't always deserved in previous eras either. But I'm sure there have been times when it was, and I was privileged to witness some of those occasions.*

*"Our deliberations today – not just our debates, but the exercise of all our responsibilities – authorizing government policies, appropriating the funds to implement them, exercising our advice and consent role – are often lively and interesting. They can be sincere and principled. But they are more partisan, more tribal more of the time than any other time I remember. Our deliberations can still be important and useful, but I think we'd all agree they haven't been overburdened by greatness lately. And right now they aren't producing much for the American people.*

*"Both sides have let this happen. Let's leave the history of who shot first to the historians. I*

*suspect they'll find we all conspired in our decline – either by deliberate actions or neglect. We've all played some role in it. Certainly I have. Sometimes, I've let my passion rule my reason. Sometimes, I made it harder to find common ground because of something harsh I said to a colleague. Sometimes, I wanted to win more for the sake of winning than to achieve a contested policy.*

*"Incremental progress, compromises that each side criticize but also accept, just plain muddling through to chip away at problems and keep our enemies from doing their worst isn't glamorous or exciting. It doesn't feel like a political triumph. But it's usually the most we can expect from our system of government, operating in a country as diverse and quarrelsome and free as ours.*

*"Considering the injustice and cruelties inflicted by autocratic governments, and how corruptible human nature can be, the problem solving our system does make possible, the fitful progress it produces, and the liberty and justice it preserves, is a magnificent achievement.*

*"Our system doesn't depend on our nobility. It accounts for our imperfections, and gives an order to our individual strivings that has helped make ours the most powerful and prosperous society on earth.  It is our responsibility to preserve that, even when it requires us to do something less satisfying than 'winning.' Even when we must give a little to get a little. Even when our efforts manage just three yards and a cloud of dust, while critics on both sides denounce us for timidity, for our failure to 'triumph.'*

*"I hope we can again rely on humility, on our need to cooperate, on our dependence on each other to learn how to trust each other again and by so doing better serve the people who elected us. Stop listening to the bombastic loudmouths on the radio and television and the Internet. To hell with them. They don't want anything done for the public good. Our incapacity is their livelihood.*

*"Let's trust each other. Let's return to regular order. We've been spinning our wheels on too many important issues because we keep trying to find a way to win without help from across the aisle. That's an approach that's been employed by both sides, mandating legislation from the top down, without any support from the other side, with all the parliamentary maneuvers that requires.*

*"We're getting nothing done. All we've really done this year is confirm Neil Gorsuch to the Supreme Court. Our healthcare insurance system is a mess. We all know it, those who support Obamacare and those who oppose it. Something has to be done. We Republicans have looked for a way to end it and replace it with something else without paying a terrible political price. We haven't found it yet, and I'm not sure we will. All we've managed to do is make more popular a policy that wasn't very popular when we started trying to get rid of it.*

*"I voted for the motion to proceed to allow debate to continue and amendments to be offered. I will not vote for the bill as it is today. It's a shell of a bill right now. We all know that. I have changes urged by my state's governor that will have to be included to earn my support for final passage of any bill. I know many of you will have to see the bill changed substantially for you to support it.*

*"We've tried to do this by coming up with a proposal behind closed doors in consultation with the administration, then springing it on skeptical members, trying to convince them it's better than nothing, asking us to swallow our doubts and force it past a unified opposition. I don't think that is going to work in the end. And it probably shouldn't.*

*"The Obama administration and congressional Democrats shouldn't have forced through Congress without any opposition support a social and economic change as massive as Obamacare. And we shouldn't do the same with ours.*

*"Why don't we try the old way of legislating in the Senate, the way our rules and customs encourage us to act. If this process ends in failure, which seem likely, then let's return to regular order.*

*"Let the Health, Education, Labor, and Pensions Committee under Chairman Alexander and Ranking Member Murray hold hearings, try to report a bill out of committee with contributions from both sides. Then bring it to the floor for amendment and debate, and see if we can pass something that will be imperfect, full of compromises, and not very pleasing to implacable partisans on either side, but that might provide workable solutions to problems Americans are struggling with today.*

*"What have we to lose by trying to work together to find those solutions? We're not getting much done apart. I don't think any of us feels very proud of our incapacity. Merely preventing your political opponents from doing what they want isn't the most inspiring work. There's greater satisfaction in respecting our differences, but not letting them prevent agreements that don't require abandonment of core principles, agreements made in good faith that help improve lives and protect the American people.*

*"The Senate is capable of that. We know that. We've seen it before. I've seen it happen many times. And the times when I was involved even in a modest way with working out a bipartisan response to a national problem or threat are the proudest moments of my career, and by far the most satisfying.*

*"This place is important. The work we do is important. Our strange rules and seemingly eccentric practices that slow our proceedings and insist on our cooperation are important. Our founders envisioned the Senate as the more deliberative, careful body that operates at a greater distance than the other body from the public passions of the hour.*

*"We are an important check on the powers of the Executive. Our consent is necessary for the President to appoint jurists and powerful government officials and in many respects to conduct foreign policy. Whether or not we are of the same party, we are not the President's subordinates. We are his equal!*

*"As his responsibilities are onerous, many and powerful, so are ours. And we play a vital role in shaping and directing the judiciary, the military, and the cabinet, in planning and supporting foreign and domestic policies. Our success in meeting all these awesome constitutional*

*obligations depends on cooperation among ourselves.*

*"The success of the Senate is important to the continued success of America. This country – this big, boisterous, brawling, intemperate, restless, striving, daring, beautiful, bountiful, brave, good and magnificent country – needs us to help it thrive. That responsibility is more important than any of our personal interests or political affiliations.*

*"We are the servants of a great nation, 'a nation conceived in liberty and dedicated to the proposition that all men are created equal.' More people have lived free and prosperous lives here than in any other nation. We have acquired unprecedented wealth and power because of our governing principles, and because our government defended those principles.*

*"America has made a greater contribution than any other nation to an international order that has liberated more people from tyranny and poverty than ever before in history. We have been the greatest example, the greatest supporter and the greatest defender of that order. We aren't afraid. "We don't covet other people's land and wealth. We don't hide behind walls. We breach them. We are a blessing to humanity.*

*"What greater cause could we hope to serve than helping keep America the strong, aspiring, inspirational beacon of liberty and defender of the dignity of all human beings and their right to freedom and equal justice? That is the cause that binds us and is so much more powerful and worthy than the small differences that divide us.*

*"What a great honor and extraordinary opportunity it is to serve in this body.*

*"It's a privilege to serve with all of you. I mean it. Many of you have reached out in the last few days with your concern and your prayers, and it means a lot to me. It really does. I've had so many people say such nice things about me recently that I think some of you must have me confused with someone else. I appreciate it though, every word, even if much of it isn't deserved.*

*"I'll be here for a few days, I hope managing the floor debate on the defense authorization bill, which, I'm proud to say is again a product of bipartisan cooperation and trust among the members of the Senate Armed Services Committee.*

*"After that, I'm going home for a while to treat my illness. I have every intention of returning here and giving many of you cause to regret all the nice things you said about me. And, I hope, to impress on you again that it is an honor to serve the American people in your company.*

*"Thank you, fellow senators.*

*"Mr. President, I yield the floor."*

So it was that Senator McCain began the biggest hypocritical pronouncement and session of the United States Senate. There is no doubt that this was a stirring and supportive statement, indicating a patriotic and compassionate sentiment in his listeners to provide support for an ailing system of Health Care. This same Health Care system that was trumpeted as the way forward and allow all Americans to continue to receive the superb health care system for which America is known worldwide but one that was about to produce catastrophic problems for a large number of the American public.

I doubt that Senator McCain will ever return to the Senate – this was his "swan song". I am sure he meant it as a triumphal oration that would go down in the annals of senate history as a final tribute to a great and innovative senator. In fact, I have great regard for Senator McCain – he is without doubt a courageous and honorable man and has in the past been a steadying and bipartisan member of an often contentious and whacky group of legislators. I am also most sympathetic to his sojourn through his harrowing fight against cancer and it is partly for this reason that I do not think that he will return to the Senate. His statement to the Senate, however, was far from senatorial especially in light of his vote on the issue three days later. Furthermore this statement was simply glitz on a worthless item to make it appear formidable and give the senate some appearance of working on something that, from the beginning, they had no intention of passing.

As I pointed out the second of these four essays:

'*A number of politicians have indicated that the issue* [of Health Care] *is "complicated" it is not, it is "impossible"!*'

I believe when President Obama first introduced the concept of Health Care for America his idea was that of a Nationalized Health Care Plan, that is a "single payer" system whereby the government was in control of all Health Care for all Americans. His introduction of the "Affordable Care Act" was simply a "stepping-stone" Act to begin the process of Nationalizing the Health Care Industry. The Act was designed to fail so that a "Health Care Emergency" could be created and the Government would need to step in and remedy the situation. This the Government did but without Hillary Clinton as President the remedy was not the remedy for which the plan called. Instead an alternate plan was created to maintain the *status quo* as much as possible and not only was this impossible to achieve but also it did not further the movement toward the socialist idea of Nationalized Health Care.

The reader may consider this a pseudo conspiracy and the thinking of an "intolerable", but I urge such a person to study the facts and monitor the issues as they emerge. I sincerely believe that we are on the verge of a socialistic style revolution whereby we become "all equal but some are more equal than others".

# "Health Care Industry

## vs.

# Health Care Service"

by

Kerry R. Scott

### <u>Addendum III</u>

09/23/2017

I wrote in the first essay on 04/28/2017 the following:

*"Simply from a realistic and practical point of view I do believe that Congress should use its "discretion" in passing a Health Care Bill on the side of the Tenth Amendment ."*

On 06/27/2017 I wrote:

*"Finally, and combining all the above into one sentence, it is too soon to try and create a federal Health Care system – let the Tenth Amendment lead the way and for now let the individual States create whatever kind of Health Care system their constituents require. Congress, retreat gracefully, and go back to your States and wait until evolution has played its part and then "return to the fray".*

The Graham Cassidy Bill was introduced as a "last ditch" effort to pass some sort of Health Care legislation which would replace the failing Affordable Health Care Act (Obama Care). This latest effort suggested that the system would be more simple by simply "block-granting" the money set aside for "Obama Care" directly to the individual States.

The particular essence of the legislation is as follows:

*Removes the penalties for the individual and employer mandate.*

*In 2027 expires the existing Obama-care funding and in the meantime funds the States directly in the form of block grants.*

*Beginning in 2020 and ending in 2026 awarding to the states federal funds to be used by each State for Health Care coverage.*

*Provides cost-sharing funds to lower the cost of some Health Care plans to Insurance Companies.*

*Provides replacement funds (that will run out in 2020) to some states that have expanded their Medicaid rolls*

*Funding for Medicaid program will starting in 2020 will be State per capita based.*

*Medicaid will be changed from an "open ended entitlement" to a capped program.*

*Removes the medical device tax.*

*Essential Health Benefits to be determined by the individual States via a waiver from the federal government.*

*States may allow Health Care Insurers make premium charges based on age via a waiver from the federal government.*

*Increases the amount individuals and families may contribute more to their Health Savings Accounts (HSAs).*

*Health Savings Account can be used to pay Health Care Insurance premiums.*

*Maintaining some Obama-care taxes and therefore creating a 2020, $146 billion fund.*

*At the discretion of the individual state allows a Medicaid work requirement.*

*Cuts federal funding for Planned Parenthood for one year commencing upon the enacting of the bill.*

It seems that this "last ditch" effort has now been itself "ditched" because certain Senators would not vote in the affirmative, there was a false deadline of September 30th 2017 for a vote and the arcane rules of the Senate require 60 affirmative votes after September 30th 2017. This, to this writer's mind is another example of the Senate's complete chaotic approach to the needs of the American people. I am by no means an advocate of passing some legislation for the sake of passing legislation but do the Republican Senators not realize that ObamaCare is failing and that if left to completely fail the democrats will step in (with a blaze of glory) saving the day with a single payer system (Nationalized Health Care); and off to a Socialized State we go!

Leading the charge to scupper the so called Graham, Cassidy Legislation were three Senators, Senator Rand Paul, Senator John McCain and Senator Susan Collins.

Senator Rand Paul was the first to indicate that he intended to vote against the bill with a simple rationale concerning his vote decision. For Senator Paul the fact that the Graham, Cassidy legislation did not repeal "ObamaCare" was his single sticking point in stopping him voting the affirmative. This rationale is negative in nature. Not voting for legislation that does not accomplish a wished for item and ignoring what the positive parts of the legislation will accomplish, is a short-sighted approach – we cannot always get everything that we want. Senator Paul's indication that this was the requirements of his constituents is spurious on its face. No individual American would willingly vote to lose his or her Health Care insurance coverage, however bad that coverage was, and would welcome a stop-gap, band-aid legislation until the final repeal could be accomplished.

In a statement Senator Rand Paul comments as follows:

*"Graham/Cassidy keeps and redistributes/spends over a trillion dollars, .....My promise to the voters was to repeal Obamacare - not block grant and keep Obamacare, If Obamacare were truly repealed, this entire trillion dollars would not be spent. This is the primary obstacle to my support, and only a significant reassessment of this trillion-dollar spending regime would get my support."*

Senator John McCain on the other hand has a different take on the Graham-Cassidy proposal as his complete statement on the issue hi-lights:

*"As I have repeatedly stressed, health care reform legislation ought to be the product of regular order in the Senate. Committees of jurisdiction should mark up legislation with input from all committee members, and send their bill to the floor for debate and amendment. That is the only way we might achieve bipartisan consensus on lasting reform, without which a policy that affects one-fifth of our economy and every single American family will be subject to reversal with every change of administration and congressional majority.*

*"I would consider supporting legislation similar to that offered by my friends Senators Graham and Cassidy were it the product of extensive hearings, debate and amendment. But that has not been the case. Instead, the specter of September 30th budget reconciliation deadline has hung over this entire process.*

*"We should not be content to pass health care legislation on a party-line basis, as Democrats did when they rammed Obamacare through Congress in 2009. If we do so, our success could be as short-lived as theirs when the political winds shift, as they regularly do. The issue is too important, and too many lives are at risk, for us to leave the American people guessing from one election to the next whether and how they will acquire health insurance. A bill of this impact requires a bipartisan approach.*

*"Senators Alexander and Murray have been negotiating in good faith to fix some of the problems with Obamacare. But I fear that the prospect of one last attempt at a strictly Republican bill has left the impression that their efforts cannot succeed. I hope they will resume their work should this last attempt at a partisan solution fail.*

*"I cannot in good conscience vote for the Graham-Cassidy proposal. I believe we could do better working together, Republicans and Democrats, and have not yet really tried. Nor could I support it without knowing how much it will cost, how it will effect insurance premiums, and how many people will be helped or hurt by it. Without a full CBO score, which won't be available by the end of the month, we won't have reliable answers to any of those questions.*

*"I take no pleasure in announcing my opposition. Far from it. The bill's authors are my dear friends, and I think the world of them. I know they are acting consistently with their beliefs and sense of what is best for the country. So am I.*

*"I hope that in the months ahead, we can join with colleagues on both sides of the aisle to arrive at a compromise solution that is acceptable to most of us, and serves the interests of Americans as best we can."*

Like Senator McCain's recent statement on the Senate floor, at first his latest statement seems reasonable – the American people certainly are owed a well thought-out and comprehensive bill that will solve the ills of the "Affordable Care Act". However the immediate concept that comes to mind is that the Republicans and, by extension, the Senate has had over seven years to come up with a comprehensive solution to our ailing Health Care Industry. As for Senate McCain's assertion that any bill should be:

*"..... the product of regular order in the Senate. Committees of jurisdiction should mark up legislation with input from all committee members, and send their bill to the floor for debate and amendment."*

When has this arcane process ever helped successful and timely passing of any bill? Furthermore he goes on to extol the virtues of the CBO (Congressional Budget Office) indicating:

*"Without a full CBO score, which won't be available by the end of the month, we won't have reliable answers to any of those questions."*

When has the CBO ever accurately projected *"reliable"* costs of any proposed bill and furthermore as they project costs over a period of years in the future their accuracy becomes a matter of "humor", i.e. "cannot pass the laugh test". This may seem harsh, but try referencing the CBO scoring of the Affordable Care Act,.

Senator McCain's statement, in essence, is simply a delaying and obstructive tactic. I really don't believe that Senator McCain wants or cares about a bipartisan bill to repeal and replace ObamaCare. His politics are such that he has no objection to a "single payer" system (Nationalized Health Care) and is quite willing for the Democrat's plan of letting ObamaCare fail to become fulfilled and then step in and support a bipartisan plan for a "single payer" system. This position of Senator McCain's is supported by his own words:

*"We should not be content to pass health care legislation on a party-line basis...."*

Perhaps the most telling of Senator McCain's statement is the following:

*"I would consider supporting legislation similar to that offered.... .... were it the product of extensive hearings, debate and amendment."*

So, taking his sentiments on their face value, it seems, that after seven years of pontificating upon the evils of ObamaCare and doing nothing to redeem the situation, Senator McCain is now of the opinion that there is a need for a deliberate and time consuming process in order to remedy a health care system that is of itself a "broken system". Although the Affordable Care bill is without merit and about to implode leaving many with inadequate or nonexistent Health Care, Senator McCain does not seem to realize that "time is of the essence" with regard to this issue and even a stop-gap bill will not gain his support. He seems determined to allow Americans to suffer in order to stop President Trump gaining any success. Shame on you Senator McCain!

Senator McCain goes on to state the following:

*"I believe we could do better working together, Republicans and Democrats, and have not yet really tried. Nor could I support it without knowing how much it will cost, how it will effect insurance premiums, and how many people will be helped or hurt by it."*

The above sounds a really fine sentiment and support of a bipartisan approach to health care. However, reading between the lines it would seem that again "time" is not an issue for Senator McCain. The present health care process could completely fall apart while the Senate awaits the information of *"how much it will cost"*, *"how it will effect(sic) insurance premiums"* and *"how many people will be helped or hurt…"*. In addition, according to his statement, Senator McCain is more interested in the Industry aspect of Health Care than he is in the Service aspect of Health Care: that is, the care the patients would receive. For Senator McCain Insurance Premiums and cost of health care seem significantly bigger priorities than patient's benefits and care.

Senator Susan Collins of Maine was the third Senator to indicate that she was going to join the "Scupper Gang". She indicates the following:

*"Sweeping reforms to our health care system and to Medicaid can't be done well in a compressed time frame, especially when the actual bill is a moving target,"*

She goes on to indicate that the bill would:

*"…open the door for states to weaken protections for people with pre-existing conditions, such as asthma, cancer, heart disease, arthritis and diabetes."*

Her first point – *"the compressed time frame"* baffles me. How is it that a seven year time frame can be considered as *"compressed"*. Her second point, *"protection of patients with pre-existing conditions"*, really indicates that Senator Collins has no faith in some state governments to provide the federal funds for those patients most vulnerable and sick. However she should be aware that State Governments are elected to their positions and are not lackeys of Washington. If Health Care block grants are made to the States for disbursement then the Federal Government has the responsibility to trust them to cater to their constituents. Although many law makers in Washington would like to deny the States their constitutional right of sovereignty, Health Care should not be the vehicle by which they try to accomplish this step toward Socialism.

The weak and poor excuses (for that is what they are – excuses!) put forward by this trio of Senators, hide, I believe, a more sinister conspiracy afoot.

While the Senate is clearly dysfunctional and chaotic with its arcane and bizarre procedural rules (none of which have any reference to the Constitution), they are responsible for passing legislation that is for the benefit of the American people; that solves past legislative problems and provides legislation that almost provides a solution prophesy for future problems.

These three senators, all trumpeting very laudable (but laughable) excuses, call themselves Republicans. But are they? They are certainly members of the Republican Party and if that is the criteria for being a Republican so be it – they are indeed Republicans. However, I believe that they can be Socialists as well as Republicans. Democrats can be Progressives as well as Socialists. The criteria is what the individual believes. If an individual believes in a central government with complete power and control over all aspects of an individual's life then even if they are a member of the Republican Party they are still Socialists. If, as has been mooted very often recently, the "two party system" is dead and America expands the political system to a multi-party system we will see many members of both the Republican and Democrat parties defect to a party that has a (probably hidden) mandate of Socialism. This has been demonstrated quite clearly in Europe where a multi-party system has existed for many years and resulted in a socialistic dysfunctional, chaotic and violent European Union.

It is a debatable point as to the true intentions of this trio of "spoilers", but what is indisputable is that these three believe in the fact that a centralized American Government is the answer, and the only answer, to ills that inhabit Health Care in America.

On Thursday October 12th 2017 President Trump signed an Executive Order that did in effect two things. Firstly it was reported that it removed the "subsidies" ObamaCare provided for the Insurance Companies in order to offset the costs of providing Health Care to those Americans who could not afford such care; secondly it provided for negotiations on Health Care across "state lines". To be honest after reading the Executive Order as published by the White House I cannot confirm that the Order did in fact remove the "subsidies" to the Insurance Companies. On the other hand it is quite clear from the document that it does provide for the purchase of Health Care Insurance across State lines.

However, what is important here is the fact that President has not given up on his push for Health Care reform. He has, it seems, given up on Congress but not on the idea that he wants to make Health Care in America better and if that means resorting to the "Executive Order" so be it.

# "Health Care Industry
## VS.

# Health Care Service"

by

Kerry R. Scott

### <u>Addendum IV</u>

*A Personal Narrative of Health Care Administrative Incompetence and Dysfunction.*

10/08/2017

My wife and I have been patients of a particular Primary Care Physician for at least 15 years; so it was significantly unfortunate that we learned through gossip and hear-say that it was being alleged that as of August 31st 2017 our PCP (Primary Care Physician) no longer was going to honor the SCO (Senior Care Options) program of a particular HMO (Health Maintenance Organization).

Both my wife and I have been most appreciative and content with our PCP's care for our health up to the point that a larger Boston based hospital took over not only the local area hospital but also all the satellite family health PCP Health Practices and Clinics. After the take-over both my wife and I noted a more controlling, arrogant and less attentive attitude of both the staff and our PCP.

About six months ago MassHealth (my secondary Health Insurer – Medicare being my primary Health Insurer) sent me a letter strongly suggesting that I sign-up for a SCO program and enclosed in the letter a number of flyers for various different programs including a flyer for the same SCO in which my wife was enrolled. Reading between the lines, I surmised that MassHeath was "outsourcing" a number of their programs with the eventual goal of terminating their involvement in various aspects of the MassHeath programs and becoming simply a re-funding agency.

We learned of the alleged termination of our PCP's contract with the SCO program as of August 2017 by mistake. I had for sometime thought of changing my MassHealth Standard to a SCO program. As my wife was already enrolled in an SCO linked to a HMO and was pleased with the program, naturally I pursued an application for enrollment in this same SCO.

Last year I had a very bad experience with the transportation portion of the MassHealth program; when I was left stranded in a wheelchair, without food, water or cell phone, for eight and half hours during a rain storm. This caused me significant emotional strain and caused me to view with trepidation further trips to medical appointments via transportation provided by MassHealth Standard.

For a significant period of time I debated with myself the various *pros and cons* of changing from MassHealth Standard to an SCO program and weighed the importance of the various benefits that both programs offered. Early in September 2017 I finally made the decision to change to the SCO in which my wife was enrolled. On Thursday September 21st 2017 at 3:00 p.m. I had the initial interview and signed the necessary application forms. One of the most important reasons for deciding to make the change to this particular SCO was that my Primary Care Physician was part of both the MassHealth Standard network as well as this particular SCO network. I should point out that I suffer from Post Polio Syndrome and that the only specialist that I am aware of on the east coast is Dr. Darren Rosenberg at the Spaulding Clinic in Framingham. Dr. Rosenberg is not part of this particular SCO's network and so my decision became between keeping my Post-Polio Syndrome doctor and suffering a very stressful transportation program or enjoying the enhanced benefits of an SCO program and removing the stress and emotional angst of medical appointment transportation. Had I realized that I would be looking for another Primary Care Physician if I changed to this particular SCO program, I would possibly have made a very different decision.

On Monday September 25th 2017 at 11:19 a.m. I received a telephone call from the HMO to confirm that I realized that in enrolling in this particular SCO and naming this particular doctor as my Primary Care Physician, I would need to obtain another primary care physician within a six month "continuity of care" period. This was because, according to the caller from the HMO, SCO, my present PCP was canceling (or not renewing?) their contract with this particular SCO as of December 2017. I immediately called my PCP and, after a period of time in which none of the staff that I spoke to seemed to know anything about the cancellation of the contract, it was confirmed that indeed the PCP was not accepting this particular SCO as of December 2017. Moreover it was also communicated to me that the after December 2017 the PCP was not accepting any SCO program at all. The staff member concerned suggested that my wife look for other Health Insurance.

On Tuesday September 26th 2017 I received another telephone call from the HMO indicating that they were incorrect in the information they had provided the day before and stated that the PCP's contract had been terminated as of the last day of August 2017 and not as of December 2017 as previously alleged. In addition, as I had not enrolled in the SCO prior to the last day of August 2017, I was not eligible for the "continuity of care" period of 6 months and if I wanted to pursue the application I had two days in which to find a new Primary Care Physician. Naturally, I withdrew my application.

On Wednesday September 27th 2017 in the late afternoon my wife and I received numerous telephone calls from the PCP's office as well as the HMO and the office of the SCO to indicate that my PCP *was* indeed part of the SCO's network. The situation, as explained to us, was that the PCP's association with a particular Physicians Association/Group was terminated upon the last day of August 2017 but on the first day of September 2017 the PCP officially joined another Physicians Association/Group. We were assured by both the PCP's office and the HMO's office that our PCP was indeed part of the SCO's network and in light of that assurance I put into operation a re-application process for the SCO.

On Thursday September 28th 2017 at 9:45 a.m., I completed, signed and submitted a second series of application forms for acceptance into the SCO to the SCO Account Executive – Senior Care Products.

On Friday September 29th 2017 (late afternoon) my wife and I received a telephone call from the HMO indicating that again they had made a mistake and that although they could confirm that our PCP had terminated their association with the first Physician's Associates group upon the last day of August 2017, there was no record of our PCP joining any other group and therefore the PCP was no longer part of the particular SCO network. In consequence, my re-application submitted the previous day had been withdrawn. We were also informed that a total of eight other Primary Care Physicians that had been part of this particular SCO network were also no longer part of the network. My wife immediately called our PCP's office manager and she promptly indicated that this was simply a paperwork delay and we should wait until the computer gets caught-up. She further pointed out that we should "wait" "about 7 to 10 working days" for resolution of the issue. Eight days into the "7 to 10 working days" we had not heard from the SCO, The HMO, The Physician's group of which our PCP is a new member, nor our PCP's former group/association. I cannot help but observe that this is not only bad business on the parts of all of those agencies but also represents a demeaning, uncaring, arrogant, controlling and rude approach toward patients and demonstrates a complete incompetence upon the part of the Health Care agencies and their staff concerned with this issue. How can we have trust and respect for any of the members of these companies when they have the temerity and gall to expect us to "wait" for an answer to a simple question of status and fact.

On Friday October 13th 2017 at 9:41 a.m. (the ninth working day of the "wait" period of 7 to 10 working days) we received a call from the HMO indicating (and apparently confirming) that the eight PCP's that were in the SCO network were no longer part of the SCO network. This, of course, was not news to us and we pointed out to the HMO staff member calling us, the information the PCP Office Manager had imparted to us on Friday September 29th 2017concerning the "wait" period for the "paper work to catch up". The HMO staff member seemed surprised at this information and indicated that she would consult her supervisor on the matter. At 10:28 a.m. the same Friday we received a telephone call from the Office Manager of our PCP indicating that indeed her information was incorrect about the "wait" period and confirmed that the PCP was not going to take any SCOs (including the SCO to which my wife belonged) after December 1st 2017. Although the information was already known to us, the date of cancellation was a real surprise. . Later that day at 3:33 p.m the PCP Office Manager called again and indicated that the information she had given was now confirmed but that the cancellation date she previously stated was incorrect, the cancellation date was September 1st 2017. The Office Manager further confirmed, therefore, that my wife had no Primary Care Physician as of that date and that all her appointments with her PCP had been cancelled. When asked about the continuation of medication scripts and refills, the Office Manager indicated that the practice would work with my wife concerning this issue. My wife is taking a de-coagulant medication and is monitored both by the PCP and an Anticoagulant clinic at the local hospital. The Office Manager seemed unclear as to the status of the clinic visits, as well as the PCP monitoring and the medication itself.

Neither my wife nor I know who or what to believe and to say that we are taken aback by this behemoth administrative chaotic approach is an understatement of gigantic proportions. What we both *do* know is that the last two weeks have been weeks of angst and stress neither of us deserve or can handle. Even after two weeks this issue still has not been resolved. However what is most distressing is that there has been no written confirmation of any change in any aspect of our Health Care Insurance or Health Care Service. No wonder the American Health Care system is in chaos – the legislators are dysfunctional, the administrators are incompetent, the doctors have lost their moral compass and the patients are receiving inadequate care and (in some cases) unnecessary procedures.

As I have not had my application accepted by the SCO, I can continue on with my existing health insurance and I confirmed this with a staff member of my PCP. My PCP is still accepting MassHealth Standard.

Unfortunately my wife is not in the same position as I am. She has been with this particular SCO for about two years and during that time she contracted Cancer. She has been looked after very well under both the PCP and SCO networks and is now Cancer free but, naturally, she is monitored regularly.

It is surely obvious to any PCP that for any patient the Primary Care Physician is the lynch-pin of their health and treatment for serious issues. For my wife and me all the doctors, treatments, tests and medications are all linked back to the Primary Care Physician. The PCP oversees and monitors all aspects of a patient's health. My wife, with the allegation that her PCP is cancelling their contract with the SCO, has a choice between transferring back to MassHealth and her PCP continuing to be her Primary Care Physician or staying with the SCO and finding a new Primary Care Physician and also possibly compromising her cancer treatment and ongoing Cancer monitoring.

Our PCP must, surely, realize the huge difficulty for either of us to find a new Primary Care Physician. In the present Health Care climate, the likely-hood of a Health Care Practice accepting as a patient, an elderly, wheelchair bound, brace wearing, polio survivor, suffering from Post Polio Syndrome, high blood pressure and high cholesterol is almost nil. The same difficulty appears for my wife, as a Cancer survivor requiring significant monitoring and other significant health issues, finding a new Primary Care Physician.

Finally I do not understand why my wife found out about the possible cancellation of the PCP/SCO contract via gossip and hearsay. Why was there no notification of the situation at all and why, if there is a cancellation of a contract by either party, was it not the first priority to inform those people most affected by the cancellation? At this point, however, there seems no clear understanding by anyone concerned with this issue as to whether any contract has been cancelled, not cancelled, re-issued or not re-issued.

Our PCP will understand if my wife and I do not congratulate the HMO, The administrators of the SCO, The Association which our PCP now belongs or the Association which our PCP formerly belonged or the Family Health Practice and our PCP, on the handling of this situation and would truly appreciate someone providing a reason why this miasma of confusion has surfaced concerning the SCO program and our PCP.